D1258254

Down to the River

SANDRA LOUISE DYAS

DOWN TO THE RIVER

Portraits of Iowa Musicians

Foreword by **CHRIS OFFUTT**

University of Iowa Press, Iowa City

A Bur Oak Book

University of Iowa Press, Iowa City 52242
Copyright © 2007 by Sandra Louise Dyas
www.uiowapress.org
All rights reserved
Printed in China

Design by Kristina Kachele Design llc

No part of this book may be reproduced or used in any form or by any
means without permission in writing from the publisher. All reasonable
steps have been taken to contact copyright holders of material used in
this book. The publisher would be pleased to make suitable arrange-
ments with any whom it has not been possible to reach.

Photo on page 76 used with the kind permission of Chris Offutt.

The University of Iowa Press is a member of Green Press Initiative
and is committed to preserving natural resources.

Printed on acid-free paper

Library of Congress Cataloging-in-Publication Data
Dyas, Sandra Louise, 1953– .
Down to the river: portraits of Iowa musicians / by Sandra Louise Dyas;
foreword by Chris Offutt.
p.   cm. —(A bur oak book)
ISBN-13: 978-0-87745-997-2 (cloth)
ISBN-10: 0-87745-997-5 (cloth)
1. Musicians—Iowa—Portraits.   I. Title.
ML87.D93 2007
780.92′2777—dc22
[B]
                                    2006032719

07 08 09 10 11 C 5 4 3 2 1

For my daughters,
Jenna Lynn and Jamie Elizabeth,
and my granddaughter,
Caroline Louise

Contents

Iowa Waltz

Chris Offutt

In 1988 I left the hills of Kentucky to attend the Iowa Writers' Workshop. I had never met another writer, and here was a town full of people who cared as deeply about literature as I did. I fell in love with everything—the pedestrian mall, the book-stores, the gentle terrain, the brick streets. Pigs browsed in the autumn cornfields beyond town. Prairie grasses and wildflowers flourished along the roadsides.

Iowa City introduced me to bars filled with writers, artists, carpenters, musicians, filmmakers, professors, doctors, mathematicians, physicists, cabbies, waitrons, housepainters, and the ubiquitous students. I embraced a life of literature and saloons, like a young artist living in Paris between the world wars, rubbing elbows with creative people. Hanging around writers made me feel smart, but hanging around musicians made me feel cool. I wanted some of their intrinsic hipness to rub off on me. I even tried to copy how they dressed, although I never achieved the sartorial splendor of Bo Ramsey or the country hip of Dave Zollo.

Every weekend, a time period that ran from Wednesday to Saturday, I gyrated on the dance floor of the local clubs, particularly the Mill and Gabe's. I listened to local singer/songwriters bravely pouring their souls into the dim confines of smoky rooms filled with sweaty dancers. Life in Iowa City meant seeing musicians perform at night, then running into them the next day at the library, the food co-op, Prairie Lights bookstore, or on the street in the midst of errands. I particularly enjoyed the free concerts by the downtown fountain, watching the musicians greet their families after performing. The festivals offered a sense of community that influenced my decision to make my home in Iowa.

The music that attracted me most is rooted in railroad songs, cowboy ballads, and plantation blues. In Iowa the roots nestle in nine feet of topsoil made of alluvial loam. Iowa music is grounded in landscape, bordered by the two great rivers of the continent. People live with hail, blizzard, tornado, flood and drought. Every six months, the outside temperature swings a hundred degrees. Iowans will help you pull your truck out of the ditch, bend the fender off the tire, and tell you where to get a good deal on a new headlight. But don't do it again, they'll tell you, try and learn from your mistakes.

My favorite Iowa music portrays the hard-luck life of someone at the end of his rope, always willing to go a little further. Embedded within each song are deep compassion and honesty. There is no judgment, just a direct depiction of lives gone awry. Iowans are willing to accept and embrace people who make mistakes, especially the kind of mistakes that everyone has made, the wrong turns that lead to others, the solutions that make problems worse. By the time I heard this music, I had spent a decade living that way myself.

Writing about music is like dancing about architecture, but the Iowa sound is distinctive—the rhythms of Rick Cicalo and Steve Hayes (better known as Rico and Chief), Bo Ramsey's haunting slide riffs, the sheer exuberance of Dave Zollo. In live shows, Dave Moore will strap an accordion to his body and play Mexican conjunto music, switch to a Czech waltz, then a zydeco tune from New Orleans. But Dave doesn't stop there. He'll stun you with a virtuoso display on the harmonica, then stick two in his mouth and play them with no hands. I have seen it, folks, and I wasn't drinking that night.

I confess to a special affinity for the music of Kevin Gordon. Originally from Louisiana, he married an Iowan and lived here several years. We were in the Workshop together, and I'll bet my bottom dollar that he's the only songwriter in Nashville with an MFA in poetry from Iowa. Kevin's craft is evident in "Lucy and Andy Drive to Arkansas," about a young couple leaving Louisiana to elope. The music soars with a rollicking optimism, while the lyrics speak of a darker future. By the end of the song, you know the marriage is doomed, but you're carried away with the infectious cheer of romantic love.

The godfather of Iowa music is the inimitable Greg Brown, whose voice rumbles like cordwood tumbling underground. He has a striking stage presence and charisma, and in live performances Greg often tells personal stories between songs. But it is his writing ability that has always captured my attention. There is never a forced rhyme or a lyric out of place. Each tiny detail evokes an entire situation.

"Poor Back Slider" is my favorite, a grand anthem of the down-and-outer who knows his life has gotten out of hand but feels powerless to intervene. One lyric chills me every time I hear it. A man sits alone in his home, having lost what he valued most:

No children's voice, no woman's touch
Just a whiskey bottle, some shotgun shells and such

The combination of despair, whiskey, and a shotgun will come to no good end. Greg's highly developed songwriting skills are evident in the next stanza. Instead of taking the narrative to its inevitable tragic end, he probes deeper into the man's late night contemplations:

The preacher told me Jesus laid down his life for my sin
Well I'd lay mine down too if I could do it like him
Three days in the grave—that sounds good to me
I just have some problems with eternity

I had never considered this perspective on our culture's most enduring story, but I am in full agreement with the idea. A three-day death is less terrifying than forever. Only the best writer can accomplish that in a few short lines—provide insight through image and deep point of view.

The Iowa sound spreads as a result of direct transmission from one musician to another. We are now seeing the second generation with Pieta Brown, who began writing poems, then learned to play guitar, and is now a veteran trouper performing her own songs around the country.

The future of Iowa music surrounds us in the public venues of coffeehouses, open microphone nights, youth centers, and high school battles of the bands. At age fourteen, my son James plays guitar every day and has for two years. He received lessons from Dustin Busch, who was himself a student of Dave Moore. James's first guitar was given to him by his former babysitter, Constie Brown, who received it in turn from her father, Greg. Like the sowing and harvest of seasonal crops, Iowa music continues to grow.

Sandy Dyas's presence at a bandshow is as natural as that of the musicians themselves. She is always there, always cheerful, and always holding a camera. No one feels uncomfortable or intimidated by her presence, and no one plays to her lens. In addition to intimate portraits, this book documents musical performances, fully embracing the cramped stages and the erratic lighting. Most of all, the photographs record the intensity of human commitment to music.

The world is a better place for the Iowa sound. The musicians are fortunate that Sandy was there. You are lucky to hold this book.

Put on the CD.

Turn it up loud.

Look at the photographs.

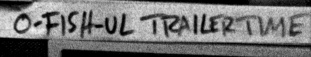

TRAILER

DOORS 7
SHOW 8

Jennifer Danielson	8 – 8:30
Pieta Brown	8:45 – 9:15
Bottle Rockets	9:30 – 10:05
Dave Zollo	10:15 – 11:00
Joe Price	11:15 – 12:00
Bo Ramsey	12:15 – 1:15

Song and Dance

Music moves me in a way that nothing else does. Since photographs and music hold both memories and ideas, they can transport the viewer or the listener to another place. I am not a musician, but I use a camera as I would play an instrument. I take my camera to clubs and concerts to be part of the music. I love the energy that grows between the musicians and the crowd in places where people are enjoying themselves and are not so conscious of my camera. Being on the dance floor with a camera . . . with the energy of the music . . . inspires my images. The energy created between the audience and the musicians builds into a crescendo, and then the night ends.

As a child, taking pictures was considered my hobby. I suppose it was not all that unusual that I dressed our barn cats in my doll clothes and took pictures of them. Later, I posed my cousins and my family and took pictures of them. Growing up on a farm in eastern Iowa was a simple pleasure. I did not have aspirations of becoming an artist or even a photographer when I was a young girl. Such ideas just did not occur to me. Still, without my realizing it, photography became my life. It became my passion. I was the girl with the camera.

By 1976, I was living and working in Bellevue, Iowa. I had a husband and a daughter. I was now bold and brave enough to think that I could be a professional photographer (without any real training) and run a full-fledged portrait studio. When you are young, anything seems possible. And it was. I photographed hundreds of high school seniors, families, and babies—and about forty weddings every year for nearly a dozen years.

In August 1981, a few months after my divorce, friends in Bellevue invited me to go to Cooper's Wagon Works in Dubuque for a night of live music and dancing. Cooper's had a small bar and a tiny dance floor and brought in a wide variety of music from all over the Midwest. That summer night we were in for a memorable treat: Bo Ramsey and the Sliders. In those days, the same band played all night. Three sets.

Over time, I was introduced to the Iowa City music scene via my acquaintance with Radoslav Lorković, who played piano and the B3 organ for the Sliders. My long-deliberated decision to leave Bellevue and my portrait studio business behind was based primarily on my desire to go back to college, but the vibrancy of Iowa City's live music scene did indeed have its own allure. In 1987, I made up my mind: I had to go. It was one of the most difficult decisions I have ever made. Starting over in Iowa City was an exciting endeavor but also quite challenging for my daughters and myself.

The 1990s were years of amazing live music in Iowa City. My friend Justine Zimmer and I would frequently divide our evenings of music and dancing between Gabe's and the now-long-gone Gunnerz. Today, times have changed. My generation of musicians is now older, and there is a new generation on the horizon—tightly connected, sometimes related by blood, but always related to the roots of a certain kind of sound: the blues and the rock-and-roll that was born from the blues, music that speaks to me like no other music can.

Since the late 1980s, I have been photographing live music venues and shooting portraits of musicians in and around Iowa City, while simultaneously working on my Lost Nation photographs, an exploration of found photographs that evoke messages of hope and hopelessness. Prior to printing my musician series, I did not see these two bodies of work as being related. But they are. In all of my photographs, there is a strong interest in the moment, in the present. My photographs are also about a sense of place and what this place means to me. The camera allows me to be intimate with the world. I want my photographs to hold the power and the honesty of real life.

These past three years have been spent working toward the publication of my first book of photographs. Looking back, going through my archives, remembering, and seeing have been quite revealing. Years have gone by, but the music and its stories still exist in my pictures. Lingering memories are all tied to nights of great music and friends . . . dancing . . . forgetting the world outside for a while. The music that I have listened and danced to has become part of me. Music, words, and pictures make an enormous difference in our lives. I hope to share my experiences through my photographs. Listen to these pictures.

Portraits of Iowa Musicians

Bo Ramsey, Lansing Music Festival, Lansing, Iowa, June 2004.

Dave Moore on the Iowa River, Johnson County, Iowa, July 1999.

Greg Brown, Iowa City, Iowa, October 1999.

Bo Ramsey (left) and Greg Brown with Steve Hayes and Rick Cicalo, City Park Music Festival, Iowa City, Iowa, July 3, 2000.

Opposite: David Zollo, City Park Music Festival, Iowa City, Iowa, July 3, 2000.

Kevin Gordon on Iowa Street, Iowa City, Iowa, winter 1991.

Greg Brown, Iowa City, Iowa, October 1999.

Pieta Brown, Iowa City, Iowa, March 2005.

Left to right: Dustin Busch, Kelly Pardekooper, Atom Robinson, and Matt Winegardner of
Kelly Pardekooper and the Devil's House Band, Johnson County, Iowa, February 2000.

Joe Price, Iowa City, Iowa, July 2000.

David Zollo, Wellman, Iowa, August 1998.

Sonny Lott, David Hazell Music Festival, Iowa City, Iowa, September 1998.

Left to right: Radoslav Lorković, David Zollo, and Dave Moore, David Hazell Music Festival, Iowa City, Iowa, September 1998.

Left to right: Marty Christensen, Bo Ramsey, Steve Hayes, and Al Schares of Bo Ramsey and the Backsliders, Iowa City, Iowa, August 1994.

Opposite: David Zollo with High and Lonesome, Gabe's, Iowa City, Iowa, 1996.

Left to right: Darren Matthews, Eric Griffin, Tom Jessen, Eric Straumanis, and
Marty Letz of Tom Jessen and the Dimestore Outfit, Iowa City, Iowa, 1995.

Tom Jessen, Oxford, Iowa, September 1996.

Joe Price on the Iowa River, Johnson County, Iowa, April 2004.

Dave Moore and Zoë on the Iowa River, Johnson County, Iowa, July 1999.

Left to right: Ed Nehring, Susie Nehring, and Jon Cummins of the Nitro Ground Shakers, Ed's Juke Joint, Iowa City, Iowa, June 1995.

Opposite: Eric Straumanis (right) and James Robinson of the Roughhousers, Ed's Juke Joint, Iowa City, Iowa, June 1995.

Tom Jessen, Iowa City, Iowa, July 2002.

Radoslav Lorković, somewhere in South Dakota, August 2003.

Kevin Gordon (center) with Rick Schell and Jim Whitfield of the Kevin Gordon Band, Gabe's, Iowa City, Iowa, July 3, 1998.

Jim Viner at the Kevin Gordon show, Gabe's, Iowa City, Iowa, July 3, 1998.

Greg Brown (left) and Joe Price, the Mill, Iowa City, Iowa, July 1999.

Opposite: Joe Price (left) and Dave Moore, the Mill, Iowa City, Iowa, July 1999.

Pieta Brown, Johnson County, Iowa, fall 2001.

Greg Brown backstage, St. Paul, Minnesota, summer 2000.

Dave Moore with the Dave Moore Band, Mondo's, Iowa City, Iowa, July 2001.

Darren Matthews (left) and Ruairi Fennessy of High and Lonesome, Gunnerz, Iowa City, Iowa, October 1996.

Radoslav Lorković, Iowa City, Iowa, September 1998.

Benson Ramsey (left) and David Huckfelt of the Pines, Johnson County, Iowa, winter 2004.

Vicki Price, Iowa City, Iowa, September 2005.

Susan Shore, Riverside, Iowa, June 1997.

Amy Finders and Mike Finders, Iowa City, Iowa, June 2005.

Joe Price and Vicki Price, Seed Savers Exchange Festival, near Decorah, Iowa, July 2004.

Kelly Pardekooper, Iowa City, Iowa, August 2004.

Teddy Morgan, Iowa City, Iowa, February 1999.

Keith Dempster (left) and Greg Brown, the Mill, Iowa City, Iowa, March 2000.

Bo Ramsey (left) and Greg Brown, the Mill, Iowa City, Iowa, March 2000.

Greg Brown (left) and Steve Hayes, Greg's last show at the Mill, July 2003.

Opposite: Sonny Lott, Mississippi Valley Blues Festival, Davenport, Iowa, July 2005.

Bo Ramsey, City Park Music Festival, Iowa City, Iowa, July 3, 2000.

Rick Cicalo, City Park Music Festival, Iowa City, Iowa, July 3, 2000.

Nate Basinger with Shame Train, Summer Concert Series, Iowa City, Iowa, July 2004.

Teddy Morgan (left, guest guitar player) and Kelly Pardekooper with Kelly Pardekooper and the Devil's House Band, Gabe's, Iowa City, Iowa, July 2002.

Pieta Brown, Coralville, Iowa, June 2003.

Bo Ramsey, Johnson County, Iowa, fall 1994.

Greg Brown, Hacklebarney, Van Buren County, Iowa, January 2004.

Left to right: Rick Cicalo, Eric Griffin, Bo Ramsey, and Radoslav Lorković of Bo Ramsey and the Sliders, Iowa City, Iowa, summer 1992.

Dave Moore with the Dave Moore Band, Kegler Lounge at Playmor Lanes, Iowa City, Iowa, March 2000.

Dustin Busch, Iowa City, Iowa, September 1998.

Left to right: Jim Viner, David Zollo, Darren Matthews, Ruairi Fennessy, and Dustin Conner of High and Lonesome, Iowa City, Iowa, June 1995.

Opposite: BeJae Fleming, Iowa City, Iowa, June 2005.

Kevin Gordon with the Kevin Gordon Band, Gabe's, Iowa City, Iowa, March 1998.

David Zollo (left) and Ruairi Fennessy, Gabe's, Iowa City, Iowa, November 1999.

Sign outside Gabe's back entrance, Iowa City, Iowa, June 1996.

Teddy Morgan with Teddy Morgan and the Pistolas, Gabe's, Iowa City, Iowa, November 1999.

Bo Ramsey with the Middle of Nowhere Band, the Green Room, Iowa City, Iowa, February 2001.

Photographer's Note

Garry Winogrand said that the kind of camera you use depends upon the kind of person you are and how you relate to the world. For Winogrand as well as many other photographers, a 35mm is the camera of choice. I like getting to know the world by using my camera. Specifically, I am most interested in people and their relationships with the world. I am immersed in the mix of life and art. There is no separation between who I am and what I do.

When I started taking my camera along with me to gigs in the late 1980s, I used an old Minolta SRT 101 from the early 1970s. It was my first SLR 35mm, and my boyfriend at the time had given it to me for Christmas. Not too long after that, we married and had two daughters. He had a guitar and I had my camera.

I still have that camera. It was used for some of my earlier photographs. Sometime in the 1990s, I bought several used SLR Minolta X-700s. About five years ago, I decided to get serious and buy a new Nikon F100. Now I have two. I thought I would like the auto focus, but I haven't really become used to that method and rely on my eye instead.

The photographs I take while on the dance floor are made with wide to normal lenses. I need fast lenses and fast film. I like to get as close as possible and don't enjoy being far away using telephoto lenses. One exception to that was a show in Minneapolis when Bo Ramsey was playing with Lucinda Williams. Bigger names, bigger shows, less access. Wide-angle lenses add a bit of image distortion and allow you to pack a lot of information into the frame. The unexpected information and the little details in the image are part of what fascinates me about capturing a moment in time. I like the challenge of using the entire frame of my negative. It is rare for me to crop my work. Only a handful of the photos in this book are cropped.

One would think I would know what kind of film I like by now. Over the years I have used Kodak TRI-X and T-MAX. Right now I prefer the TRI-X. For live shows and also for many of the portraits, I prefer to use 400-speed film. If I want to attain less depth of field in a portrait and less grain, I will use a slower film speed. It just depends on what I am looking for and what the lighting situation is. If I can, I like to use the available and/or natural light. Sometimes I push the film to 1600 if the lighting insists on it. I have also used 3200-speed film; this film is hit or miss. Lighting is key to my response as an artist. Gabe's in Iowa City has been my favorite environment for live shots of musicians because it has the best lighting (as well as the best dance floor). The atmosphere in Gabe's adds a great ambience to the photo as well. Slow shutter speeds can enhance the photo's feel as they result in a blurred image, a nice way to view the world. Occasionally I use a flash, a necessary device when the lighting just isn't good enough.

Not being overly concerned with film or camera gear can be troublesome, but it has ultimately resulted in a personal style. If you are a film photographer and not a digital photographer, then you must be open to surprises. As my photographer friend Eugenia Uhl says, if you shoot film, you must always pray to the film gods. You can never be sure what you are getting on film. Sometimes what you think is an amazing shot turns out to lack what you thought it had. And then there are the times when you see an image on your contact sheet and you are knocked out.

Several years ago, the *Icon*, an alternative newspaper in Iowa City, wanted to do a photo spread of my musician work, so I began digging through my archives. As

I selected the images for this book, I printed my negatives onto fiber paper for the first time, making fine silver gelatin prints of each chosen negative. The 11-by-14-inch Agfa multicontrast, glossy fiber paper, which unfortunately is no longer available, is wonderfully rich in its black and white tones.

After my final prints were made, I made photocopies of each one and began laying out the images to give me a hands-on idea of how the book might eventually look. It also gave me a much clearer sense of how the photographs were interrelated, which ones needed to be in the book, and which could be omitted. A workshop by Sylvia Plachy gave me insight into the importance of pairing photographs. Selecting the songs and sequencing them for the CD was a similar endeavor. I listened carefully to the way each song sounded when heard in a given order. Each song, like each photograph, had a particular mood and composition; careful attendance to this created continuity as I strung them together to construct something bigger.

For me, the best part of being a photographer is taking the image. I can leave exposed film sitting around for months. I realize that is not good, but it is what I do. It takes a great deal of time to print and then there is the endless editing. I hesitate to admit just how long it took me to select the final images for this book. Printing later gives me time to reflect on the individual images once they are contacted. Going over my contact sheets from the early 1990s was interesting. I see things now that I would not have seen then.

The commissioned portraits included in this book were taken with several cameras. Depending upon the situation, I generally use my 35mm cameras, but at times I choose to use a medium-format camera. I love the large negative, but you must use a tripod with the Mamiya RB67, so the working method is quite different; it is a much slower process. I spend much more time thinking about the image and am not so quick to snap the shutter. My medium-format cameras are a Mamiya 645 and a Mamiya RB67. Unlike the other commissioned photographs included in this book, my newest portrait of Radoslav Lorković on the road in South Dakota was taken with a Holga, a cheap plastic camera that uses medium-format film. I like its unpredictability. Sylvia Plachy told me that the Holga is the only camera that comes with a soul.

This book of photographs contains only my black and white work. I also have a fair number of color photographs of the musicians, but I prefer the timelessness of black and white photography. Darkroom work is not my favorite part of being an image maker, but I do enjoy the magic that happens there, even though it keeps me downstairs in my darkroom . . . rather than on the dance floor.

Acknowledgments

I want to thank every one of my musician friends for the music that inspired these photographs and for their kind words of support throughout this project.

David Zollo has been a big part of this project. Thank you, David, for your friendship, for including me in the Trailer Records family, and for everything you did to make the *Down to the River* CD possible.

A very, very large thank-you goes to the Iowa Arts Council for its generous project grant, which gave me both financial support and a great deal of confidence as an artist.

My friend Justine Zimmer deserves a special thank-you too. She and I spent many good times together listening to music, driving to festivals, and staying up way too late—lots of good memories go along with those wonderful years of listening to music and dancing with our friends.

If it were not for Justine's sincere encouragement, I might not have shown Holly Carver, my editor and publisher, this body of photographs. Thank you, Holly, for your encouragement, patience, and support; you gave me a heightened awareness of the historical importance of documenting the music scene in Iowa City.

I want to thank Chris Offutt, my good friend and fellow artist, for his friendship and generosity.

To my daughters, Jenna Lynn and Jamie Elizabeth, and my granddaughter, Caroline Louise, I send my love.

K 400TX   15   KODAK 400TX   16   KODAK 400TX   17   KODAK 400TX   18   KODAK 400TX   19

14A   15   15A   16   16A   17   17A   18   18A   19

25   KODAK 400TX   26   KODAK 400TX   27   KODAK 400TX   28   KODAK 400TX   29   KO

7   25   25A   26   26A   27   27A   28   28A   29

1   2   KODAK 5053 TMY   3   KODAK 5053 TMY   4   KODAK 5053 TMY   5

0A   1   1A   2   2A   3   3A   4   4A   5

MZ   25   KODAK 5054 TMZ   26   KODAK 5054 TMZ   27   KODAK 5054 TMZ   28   KODAK 5054 TMZ   29   K

   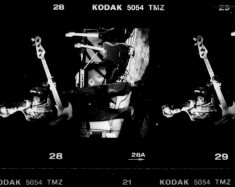

25   25A   26   26A   27   27A   28   28A   29

KODAK 5054 TMZ   19   KODAK 5054 TMZ   20   KODAK 5054 TMZ   21   KODAK 5054 TMZ

18A   19   19A   20   20A   21   21A

CD Tracks and Credits

Heartfelt thanks to the following musicians, who generously gave me permission to include their songs and performances on this CD.

1. **IOWA CRAWL**, Joe Price   4:00
   Song written by Joe Price
   Joe Price: vocals and guitar
   Keni Ewing: drums
   Radoslav Lorković: accordion
   Vicki Price: back-up vocals
   Bo Ramsey: back-up vocals
   Mark Stumme: bass

From *Requests*, Trailer Records, 1999. Produced by Joe Price. Recorded by Mark Stumme. Mixed by Bo Ramsey, Mark Stumme, and Joe Price at Radon Studio, Decorah, Iowa. For more information visit www.trailer-records.com and www.joepriceblues.com.

2. **POOR BACK SLIDER**, Greg Brown   4:06
   Song written by Greg Brown
   Greg Brown: vocals and guitar
   Angus Foster: bass
   Steve Hayes: drums
   Bo Ramsey: guitar and back-up vocals

From *Down in There*, Red House Records, Inc., 1990. Produced by Bo Ramsey, Greg Brown, and Bob Feldman at Metro Studios, Minneapolis, Minnesota. Engineered by Tom Tucker. For more information visit www.redhouserecords.com and www.gregbrown.org.

3. **PARNELL**, David Zollo   4:11
Song written by David Zollo
David Zollo: vocals and piano
Andy Carlson: guitar, fiddle, and mandolin
Marty Christensen: bass
Eric Griffin: drums and percussion
Bo Ramsey: guitar and back-up vocals

From *Uneasy Street*, Trailer Records, 1998. Produced by David Zollo and John Svec. Recorded and mixed at Minstrel Studios, Iowa City, Iowa. Mastered by Jon Chamberlain at Catamount Recording, Cedar Falls, Iowa. For more information visit www.trailer-records.com and www.davidzollo.com.

4. **#807**, Pieta Brown   3:33
Song written by Pieta Brown (Woo Jones Music/BMI)
Pieta Brown: vocals and guitar
Dave Jacques: bass
Bryan Owings: drums
Bo Ramsey: guitar

From *In the Cool*, Valley Entertainment, Inc., 2005. Produced by Bo Ramsey and Pieta Brown. Recorded by John Hampton at Ardent Studios, Memphis, Tennessee. Mixed by Tom Tucker. For more information visit www.pietabrown.com.

5. **WHEELS OF STEEL**, Radoslav Lorković   4:13
Song written by Radoslav Lorković
Radoslav Lorković: vocals, piano, and accordion
Lee Zimmerman: cello

From *Blue Parade*, Hot Spring Records, 2005. Produced by Radoslav Lorković and Lee Zimmerman. Recorded at First United Methodist Church, Missoula, Montana. Engineered by Lee Zimmerman. Mixed by Lars-Erik Pointer at Cougar Canyon Studio, Woods Bay, Montana. For more information visit www.radoslavlorkovic.com.

6. **DOWN TO THE RIVER**, Dave Moore   3:32
Song written by Dave Moore and Josie Moore (BMI)

Dave Moore: vocals and guitar
Rick Cicalo: bass
Steve Hayes: drums
Bo Ramsey: guitar and back-up vocals

From *Breaking Down to Three*, Red House Records, Inc., 1999. Produced by Bo Ramsey and Dave Moore. Recorded by Brent Sigmeth at Pachyderm Studio, Cannon Falls, Minnesota. Mixed by Tom Tucker at Oar Fin Studios, Minneapolis, Minnesota. Mastered by David Glasser at Airshow Mastering, Boulder, Colorado. For more information visit www.redhouserecords.com.

7. **LUCY AND ANDY DRIVE TO ARKANSAS**, Kevin Gordon   3:42
   Song written by Kevin Gordon (Kevin Gordon Music/BMI)
   Kevin Gordon: vocals and guitar
   Steve Hayes: drums and percussion
   Mitchell Moss: fiddle and back-up vocals
   Mike Murray: bass

From *Carnival Time*, Maverick Music, 1993. Produced by Kevin Gordon and Bo Ramsey for Shed Records. Recorded by Tom Tatman and John Thomson at Catamount Recording, Cedar Falls, Iowa. For more information visit www.kevingordon.net.

8. **CHUCK BROWN**, Mike and Amy Finders   4:02
   Song written by Mike Finders (© 2003 Hickory Doodle Music/BMI)
   Mike Finders: vocals and guitar
   Amy Finders: vocals and mandolin
   Dustin Busch: Dobro
   Billy Valencia: bass

From *Where You Are*, Neighborly Records, 2004. Produced by Mike Finders, Amy Finders, and Patrick Brickel. Engineered, mixed, and mastered by Patrick Brickel at PZM Studios, Iowa City, Iowa. For more information visit www.mikeandamyfinders.com.

9. **NOBODY BUT YOU**, Joe Price   2:59
   Song written by Joe Price
   Joe Price: vocals and guitar with the Trailer Trillionaires
   Rick Cicalo: bass
   Vicki Price: guitar and back-up vocals
   Bo Ramsey: guitar
   Jim Viner: drums
   David Zollo: piano

From *Designated Driver*, Trailer Records, 2000. Produced by Bo Ramsey. Recorded at the Petting Zoo, Iowa City, Iowa. Engineered by Patrick Brickel. Mixed and mastered by Jeff Cozy at Bright Ideas Studios, La Crosse, Wisconsin. For more information visit www.trailer-records.com and www.joepriceblues.com.

10. **EARLETON**, BeJae Fleming 3:25
    Song written by BeJae Fleming (Utopia Road Music/BMI)
    BeJae Fleming: vocals and guitar
    Jackie Blount: bass
    Patrick Brickel: percussion
    Al Clarke: guitar
    Steve Hayes: drums
    David Zollo: keyboards

From *Destination Unimportant*, Trailer Records, 2005. Produced by David Zollo. Recorded, mixed, and mastered by Patrick Brickel at PZM Studios, Iowa City, Iowa. For more information visit www.trailer-records.com.

11. **CEREMONIAL CHILD**, High and Lonesome 3:05
    Song written by David Zollo
    David Zollo: vocals and piano
    Dustin Conner: bass
    Darren Matthews: guitar
    Dave Moore: accordion
    Bo Ramsey: guitar and back-up vocals
    Jim Viner: drums

From *For Sale or Rent*, Trailer Records, 1996. Produced by David Zollo, Bo Ramsey, and John Svec. Recorded and mixed by John Svec at Minstrel Studios, Iowa City, Iowa. Mastered by John Gohman. For more information visit www.trailer-records.com and www.davidzollo.com.

12. **SIDETRACK LOUNGE**, Bo Ramsey 4:54
    Song written by Robert Franklin Ramsey
    Bo Ramsey: vocals and guitar
    Rob Arthur: Hammond B3
    Rick Cicalo: bass
    Eric Griffin: percussion
    Bryan Owings: drums

From *In the Weeds*, Trailer Records, 2002. Produced by Bo Ramsey. Recorded by David Streeby and mixed by Tom Tucker at Oar Fin Studios, Minneapolis, Minnesota. Mastered by David Streeby. For more information visit www.trailer-records.com and www.boramsey.com.

13. **ON THE EDGE**, Pieta Brown   4:32
    Song written by Pieta Brown (Woo Jones Music/BMI)
    Pieta Brown: vocals and guitar
    Rick Cicalo: bass
    Don Heffington: drums and percussion
    Bo Ramsey: guitar

From *Pieta Brown*, Trailer Records, 2002. Produced by Bo Ramsey and Pieta Brown. Recorded by Brent Sigmeth at Pachyderm Studio, Cannon Falls, Minnesota. Mixed by Tom Tucker. For more information visit www.trailer-records.com and www.pietabrown.com.

14. **ONE WRONG TURN**, Greg Brown   3:45
    Song written by Greg Brown
    Greg Brown: vocals and guitar
    Steve Hayes: drums
    Gordy Johnson: bass
    Bo Ramsey: guitar

From *The Poet Game*, Red House Records, Inc., 1994. Produced and mixed by Greg Brown, Bo Ramsey, and Bob Feldman. Recorded at Paisley Park Studios, Chanhassen, Minnesota. Engineered by Tom Tucker. For more information visit www.redhouserecords.com and www.gregbrown.org.

15. **NOT IN IOWA**, Kelly Pardekooper   4:15
    Song written by Kelly Pardekooper
    Kelly Pardekooper: vocals and guitar
    Dave Moore: accordion
    Eric Straumanis: guitar
    John Svec: bass
    Matt Winegardner: drums

From *Haymaker Heart*, Leisure Time Records, 2005. Produced by Kelly Pardekooper and John Svec. Recorded, mixed, and mastered by John Svec at Minstrel Studios, Iowa City, Iowa. For more information visit www.kellyp.net.

16. **LIVING IN A CORNFIELD**, Bo Ramsey   5:05
    Song written by Robert Franklin Ramsey
    Bo Ramsey: vocals and guitar
    Marty Christensen: bass
    Eric Griffin: percussion
    Bryan Owings: drums
    David Zollo: piano

From *In the Weeds*, Trailer Records, 2002. Produced by Bo Ramsey. Recorded by David Streeby and mixed by Tom Tucker at Oar Fin Studios, Minneapolis, Minnesota. Mastered by David Streeby. For more information visit www.trailer-records.com and www.boramsey.com.

17. **'57 CHEVY**, Tom Jessen's Dimestore Outfit   3:01
    Song written by Tom Jessen
    Tom Jessen: vocals and guitar
    Eric Griffin: drums, percussion, and back-up vocals
    Marty Letz: guitar
    Darren Matthews: guitar
    Eric Straumanis: bass

From *Redemption*, Trailer Records, 1996. Produced by John Svec and Tom Jessen. Recorded and mixed at Minstrel Studios, Iowa City, Iowa. For more information visit www.trailer-records.com and www.tomjessen.com.

18. **ROLL ON JOHN**, the Pines   4:20
    Traditional song arranged by Benson Ramsey
    Benson Ramsey: vocals and guitar
    Constie Brown: back-up vocals
    Pieta Brown: back-up vocals
    Rick Cicalo: bass
    Brad Engeldinger: drums
    Tim Ferrin: back-up vocals
    David Huckfelt: guitar and back-up vocals
    Bo Ramsey: guitar and back-up vocals
    David Zollo: organ and back-up vocals

From *The Pines*, Trailer Records, 2004. Executive producer: Bo Ramsey. Produced by David Zollo and the Pines. Recorded, engineered, and mastered by John Svec at PZM Studios, Iowa City, Iowa. For more information visit www.trailer-records.com and www.thepinesmusic.com.